unrequited love
and other poems on life©

by Elliot M. Rubin

Copyright December 2018
Library of Congress

ISBN 978-1-7328493-1-0

   No part of this book may be reproduced in any form whatsoever without prior, express written consent of the author.
   This book is fiction, and all names, people, places, and happenings are from the author's imagination and are used fictionally.
   Any resemblance to any living or dead persons, and/or businesses, locations and/or events are coincidental in its entirety.
   All rights reserved

Dedication
To Shane, Izzy, Jon, Carter,
Alex, Melanie, Mollie and Madison

In Memory of
Herman S. Rubin
Who wrote poetry all his life.

Preface
A book of poetry can cover a lot of subjects.
Truth hurts sometimes but can also be healing
I hope you enjoy the poems.

Table of Contents

unrequited love 7
a candy call 8
the end of times 9
The Grand Concourse - The Bronx 10
Irving the Litvak 12
squiggly lines 13
lucky 7's 14
baseball 16
the line 17
senior adventures 18
our song 19
today 20
problems with marriage 21
the happiest place on Earth 22
flu season 23
finding a perfect bargain 24
Perth Amboy walk by 25
a disgusting man 26
her skin, her way, every way 27
match made in Heaven 28
forever in love 30
if Dr. Seuss wrote this poem 31
what goes around 32
waiting 34
just a wave 35
classroom lights 36

early today 37
visit to the cemetery 38
pre-winter 39
my new jacket 40
nature 41
are there still ten? 42
death 44
Saturday 45
for my bride 46
illness 47
60's flower child 48
extraction day - a circle of life 49
funeral for Farley 50
one day's mail 52
driving for romance 53
about her brother 54
Sunday shopping 55
she's dating again 56
after all these years 57
the moth, the woman, and me 58
December 24th 60
a kiss 62
absurdity 64

unrequited love

i'll be here to hold you up
if you ever crumble down

loving you from afar,
fearing rejection if I come too close,
exposing my heart to collapse
and my soul to humiliation,
leaves me on the sidelines
of love

in solitude

waiting for your call,

waiting forever,

waiting…

for you to need me

a candy call

he dialed his buddy
one afternoon to meet
after work for dinner

a sweet girl's voice
answered hello instead,
unexpectedly,
taking him somewhat back,
not understanding
who is answering

finally asking
and being told he misdialed
he apologized-
then a conversation
easily started to flow

one hour later
a date to meet
was set for coffee

this was a pleasant surprise,
like a Cracker Jack phone call.

the end of times

deep in the bowels of Hades
a creature is incubated
in searing flames, burnishing
it's soul, immunizing it from empathy

the spawn of Satan and Lilith
is regurgitated upward,
out of the underworld to
flay the earth with horror

it slimes everything,
casting off a repulsive stench
growing stronger
with every ill will
flowing from its mouth

unbeknownst to humanity
it is cloaked in deception,
taken close to the bosom of
a minor part of society,
then finally exposed -
as our illustrious president

The Grand Concourse - The Bronx

going to Yankee Stadium
we parked
near 161st Street,
then walked
to the game,
up hills,
then more hills,
till i crossed
six lanes of traffic

looking at the area
i am reminded
of an elderly queen,
still looking regal
but aged,
unsightly
from years of
wear, tear and stress;
it's front entries gated
with steel fences like a fort

a knave is laying on a doorstep
wine bottle still in hand,
his head resting
on the first concrete step
blocking the door,
while knights in blue,
standing on the corners
ignore him,
looking
at wenches
strutting
on the median
wearing skimpy skirts

and tight tube tops
with iridescent colors
waiting to party

two blocks away
the old dame's
jewel in the crown
was replaced
with a new diamond

glittering at night,
white and bright,
hoping to make the area
gleam again

but an aged queen
cannot be young again,
until she is replaced
by rehabilitated princesses

Irving the Litvak

he was a typical old-time
New York cabby
wearing a newsboy cap,
always two days of unshaved stubble
on his face with three inches
left on a chewed cigar
dangling from his lips,
speaking with a gravelly voice
is how he is remembered

he was my uncle's brother-in-law.

since my uncle didn't drive
he drove him around
to visit his sister, my grandmother

the Litvak was an older, burned out
city hack driver who years later,
i learned,
charged my uncle a fare
even though it was on a Sunday,
and their wives were
always with them

our encounters never lasted more
then fifteen minutes or so
when my uncle visited;
the Litvak's taxi downstairs
still had the meter running

so much for a warm
congenial,
extended family gathering

squiggly lines

looking out the window after a rain
i see a small river of water
flowing fast,
just past my driveway,
pouring into the sewer drain
down the block

later the sun peeked out

i decided to go for a walk
when i noticed in front of
my door, under a portico,
a handful of squiggly lines
on the ice cold grey concrete

not moving, still as death,
i looked at them

escaping from drenched
soil to high dry land,
the worms died trying to avoid death

not unlike
the women and children
coming here
to escape murderous
environments-
but killed or blocked
on their way to America
by untold dangers,
or by our border guards

when all they want
to do is live

lucky 7's

arriving in Las Vegas at dusk,
my watch is reset to their time,
then i settle into a hotel room
and went downstairs to eat

finished, i enter the casino to play
an inter-connected million dollar slot machine,
enjoy free Piña Coladas,
watch ample waitresses
in low cut bustiers
walking by
getting tipped ten dollar chips

the seven keeps popping up
two or three in a row,
then on the next roll one seven and a cherry,
always winning something
with bells ringing out
and the sound of
nonexistent coins
falling into a
metal tray, there for show only,
but not the big jackpot
of four sevens in a row
and a few million dollars won

seeing my winnings
rack up big time
a lady approaches
whispering
in my left ear,
if i want to party with her

no thank you,

my machine is hot
i wanted to be cool

so am i
she said

i'm married,
very tired,
it's way past midnight,
plus i didn't want to indulge
and bring home
an incurable
Vegas memory

i need to get up early
for seminars
so i cash out,
go to bed,
return the next night
to a freezing,
ice cold,
no payout
slot machine

billion dollar Vegas casinos
are not built on money
from winners

baseball

it's been fifty years since
i attended a baseball game
at Yankee Stadium

as a Brooklyn Dodger fan
going to the Bronx was
anathema to me

as a kid, i hated the Yankees;
it was expected of us,
plus a tedious subway ride for
hours on end from Brooklyn

so i'm now sitting in the bleachers
with my friends from Jersey who took me there,
when a woman walks in the row in front
and trips falling between the rows,
still grasping some money in her hand;
not willing to lose the chance to buy
food at the concessions

on the way home I remember
the hotdog I ate better than the game…
it kept repeating!

and *i still hate the Yankees*

the line

the line of traffic on the
one lane country road
in front of me must
be over a hundred cars long,
with trucks interspersed
amongst them,
pausing for the only
traffic light
for miles around to change

robots have it better than us,
they can stand for hours not fatigued
while we are impatient,
waiting,
following
until there is a movement

the long line reminds me
of a column of ants
snaking through the
grass going wherever
the lead bug in front
is heading,
blindly following
the one in front going to work,
as I am doing to the
cars ahead of me
on this isolated
single strip of black asphalt
in the middle of nowhere

sometimes, i see no difference
between humans and ants

senior adventures

living here is dangerous,
too many elderly people
driving who shouldn't be

yet i continue to go for walks
in the street, since there are no
sidewalks, just lawns

last week an old man left
his friend's house and
stepped on the gas
smashing into
the garage door, then
slamming into the car
parked inside

not finished driving,
he puts his car in reverse,
steps on the gas
going backward down the street,
forcing a van to veer off the road
to avoid hitting him

the man eventually stops
when he drives over a wooden
mailbox and knocking over
a lamppost onto his car

thinking about this,
i realize,
in real time,
i am living in an amusement park
bumper car ride

our song

the music of my teenage years
brings back memories
of summers past-
young love lost long ago
except in my heart

when our song plays
on the radio,
the one which we slow danced
the night away,
reminds me life flies past
without us realizing
it is gone

i remember
high school graduation,
holding your hand
walking to the soda shop
to celebrate,
our parents so happy for us

life moves on,
we did too

without each other

youth vanishes,
melodies change,
old age creeps up;
where did our life go?

today

the temperature outside
is perfect,
not too cool,
not too hot,
a little breeze
fluffing leaves
making trees
wave to me,
while I walk by
early in the morning

the incline of the street increases
my heartbeat as I struggle to
clear the crest,
then ease
my way
back down the hill,
shuffling slowly
to my house

although I'm in New Jersey,
my mind feels like it's in
San Francisco

what a wonderful day

problems with marriage

this major question
is as old as which came first,
the chicken or the egg?

does the toilet paper
roll over or under?
is the question of the day

the original patent
for the paper roller
conclusively states
in words and drawing,
the paper rolls over,
but some people,
without naming names,
they remain unconvinced

then there is the issue of
up or down;
should a man lower the
seat after finishing,
or should the woman
raise the position after use?

what happened to equality?

the happiest place on Earth

the rides in Disney World
are a lot of fun
my two granddaughters
enjoyed it,
i loved
watching them smile,
laugh,
run around
after one another
as we walked along

after one short ride
in a large boat
at the Mexican pavilion,
i was walking out
and saw a teenage girl
in a reclining type
of wheelchair,
covered in blankets
with oxygen tubes poking out,
and a blank glaze
on her face;
there with her parents
and siblings

upon spotting her
my heart broke

i felt so lucky.
i felt so sad.
i felt so helpless.

i have no answers

flu season

sitting in the waiting area
of the emergency room
for my wife to be called in,
there are two late twenty-something girls
sitting across, and to my right

roly-poly friends with double chins
and an oval shape if they stood straight,
each intently looking at their phone,
ignoring
the world around them

the bigger one on the left
had a large blue cross,
set on a field of leaves
tattooed on her thick forearm,
wearing a short sleeve blouse
for all to see on a cold Autumn evening;
immune to the chilling weather

her friend wore a sweat suit
with a row of small earrings
going up her left ear,
on the rim outlining it,
somewhat pointing down
to small sweat stains
by her armpits

called to go in we walk
past them as they both cough
with a thick, hearty, hacking cough

not that i am a hypochondriac,
but i'm now waiting to get the flu

finding a perfect bargain

people are walking in the overcrowded mall
with shoppers looking for a bargain,
half off, seventy off,
and free offers

creating a frenzy of credit card waving
buyers frothing at the mouth,
rushing to the cash register
to make their purchase

i watch with amusement,
knowing in five days most of them will be back
to exchange or return what they bought,
only to re-enter the mall's aisles
to again shop for the missed savings

the similarity to marriage is striking

people rush to find the right person
then marry them;
over fifty percent
divorce

in the end they start the dating
process all over again

searching for the right one,

the best bargain to keep

Perth Amboy walk by

standing by the front of my building
as the locksmith is fixing the door,
a young olive-skinned woman walks by,
maybe in her early twenties or so,
eating cheese from an open waxed paper
smiling at me as i wave hello to her

at ten in the morning she is dressed to kill;
spandex leggings and a colorful fluffy blouse
as if it was evening, and is ready to party.
spotting me, she walks over and extends her
hand asking if I would like some cheese

i am struck by her face,
thin, a little too much eyeshadow,
with a smile from ear to ear
creating a sultry and enticing aura

i decline her offer politely,
she wishes me a good day
and continues on her walk.

i never saw her before, or after, that day;
but i always wondered where she was going,
for pleasure or for business?
either way i am sure it will be for both;
she did not look like a housewife
out for a stroll
in a quiet residential neighborhood

a disgusting man

he presses against her
stop!
she tries to push
him away

i mean it
stop!
get off me
he backs up

satisfied
with the unwanted
kiss he stole
he smiles, grinning

speechless,
in shock,
she stood there
staring at him

it can happen
anywhere,
to any woman
with no warning

stop
means
no

except
if you are
famous and rich?

yet, apparently, not too many care

her skin, her way, every way

the bright multi-colored floral tattoo
on her shoulder shouts out
to look at her,
not her body
in a skimpy two-piece swimsuit
running on the beach,
but at her shoulder,
the left one facing me
in the commercial i am watching

years ago her body would be
the attraction for men,
but times have changed,
styles have changed,
attitudes have changed

today it is not the province
of only men to ink their bodies,
it is her skin, her way of expression,
her authority over her body
in more ways than one,
and nobody has the right
to tell her otherwise

especially
flaccid,
impotent,
old men;
whose virility
waned years ago,
still passing laws
about women's bodies

match made in Heaven

watching old black and white
Hollywood movies,
a glamorous platinum blond
is sitting on a plush velvet bench,
wearing an almost sheer negligée
taking out a fashionable cigarette case
and lighting one up,
inhaling a long,
drawn-out breath,
then exhaling gray smoke
for the camera to catch mid-air
as she turns her head,
smiling at the handsome leading man
standing in her bedroom
wearing a tuxedo

the reality both then and now
is not a fancy Beverly Hills mansion,
but a trailer home
somewhere in middle America
with a hungover brunette,
with tussled stringy hair
wearing an old,
stained
man's shirt
sitting in the middle
of a rumpled bed,
with a mangy looking dog
sleeping
on the linoleum floor
drooling

her guest for the night
is pulling on his pants

while looking for one shoe

while she asks
if you call me
we can go out again

they met last night at a bar,
danced, drank and shot pool together
till the wee hours of the morning

only to find himself
in her bed
when he awoke
as the sun shined in
through stained and torn
yellowed window shades

yes, of course, I'll call you;

what's your name again?

forever in love

it was only a year ago,
but it seems like forever
my world has changed,
everything has changed,
since i lost you

the red tulips in the blue vase
you used to place on the
checkboard tablecloth
in our kitchen,
i miss seeing them every morning

the scent of your hair
when i held you in my arms
is gone,
missing from my life,
while I hold your memories
in my heart

i look forward to
walking on the clouds with you,
seeing your smile,
feeling your kindness,
now only sensing it
when i turn over in bed,
resting my head
on your pillow at night

someday,
we will be together again;
impatiently,
i wait for eternal sleep

if Dr. Seuss wrote this poem

this poem is for the poet Bill,
i wrote it on a window sill

in the village of Poetville
and counted every syllable

some write poems which rhyme,
some don't, not a crime

don't think i have the time,
think I'd just rather mime!

what goes around

as a senior in high school
i took a morning summer
speed reading course at NYU

the hot sun was burning;
i took the bus in
from our vacation home
in the Jersey mountains

after it was done,
there was time
so i walked to a small diner
in Greenwich Village
for a burger and fries

sitting in a booth by myself
looking out the window,
this plump blond girl walks over
and addresses me by name

sitting down uninvited
she informs me we went
to middle school together
years ago,
and starts a frivolous
conversation

i remember her as skinny,
and one of the in-crowd
girls who ignored me;
they were the cool ones

today she is chunky,
i no longer am,

now i'm the skinny one
making light of her smiles,
ignoring
the come-ons
eating a burger with fries
while looking at my watch,
ready to catch a bus
uptown at the Port Authority
bus terminal
back out of the city

waiting

waiting…
    always waiting,
someday i won't need to wait,
    everything will be on time

maybe…

waiting for that phone call,
waiting for the delayed train,
waiting for the receptionist to stop chewing,
waiting for the next appointment,
waiting for the next class to begin

waiting for weekends,
    they end too soon

waiting for kindness to others,
waiting for empathy to take hold,
waiting for a government that
    values people over money

waiting…

i'm forever waiting

just a wave

living in an age-restricted area
you see seniors
at all later stages of life;
many have live-in home aids

the elderly man who lives across
from my house has been out only once
since I moved in, six months ago

i see his aid walking each morning
and late afternoon
by herself,
never with him

last week i passed
his house
and she was sitting
on a folding chair
in the driveway
waving hello with a smile

today, i saw police cars
park in front, and escort her
out in handcuffs

seems he died
months ago;
she never bothered
to report it

he set up auto pay
with his bank,
and she wanted to
continue getting a salary

classroom lights

he is the tallest in the class
on the first day of school,
when in single file the students
enter walking past the nun

being the last one passing her
she grabs him by his shirt,
lifting him in the air and
pressing his back against the wall

i've heard about you,
there are no troublemakers in
my class; the only sound to be heard
is the hum from the fluorescent lights

as the tallest student,
he is seated
in the last row,
far from the front,
far from the nun,
who is sitting at her desk;
when she hears a loud hum,
and sees him smiling

early today

this morning
on my early walk
when the mist
gently kissed my face;
i decided to turn around
and go home, too wet outside

i couldn't see it
but felt the wetness

this made me uncomfortable;
not the morning chill
or the cloudy sky
but the minuscule beads
of moisture on my brow

in the warm comfort of home
i see on the news
thousands of mothers
marching slowly
hundreds of miles to America;
suckling their infants
in their arms
as they walk
in hope of a better life
for their children,
while carrying
all their possessions
on their back

i feel ashamed
to complain about
a light morning mist
on my face

visit to the cemetery

on a windy November morning,
a bone-chilling gust slams into me
as i stand on an open field in a cemetery
when i turn my head
looking at an isolated grave nearby

the grey stone monument
tells me her name
and her date of death;
an eighteen-month-old girl lies there

her grave stands alone,
not amongst the others
in the packed cemetery;
the rest of the plots
for thirty feet around
are all fallow,
empty, not filled

where are her family
members buried?
she was interred here
seventy years ago,
yet there are no others
keeping her company

she is somebody's daughter,
but whose i may never know;
yet every year i place
a single stone on her grave
and say a prayer,
because somebody
has to remember her

pre-winter

the dew of summer is gone
as ice crystals form a white,
light glaze on the bending
blades of grass,
announcing the coming
winter weather

deep in the hardening ground
rabbits are digging
their burrows,
preparing
for the December snows

stripped naked of their
green leaves,
tree limbs stretch out
like fingers
reaching into the clouds

while winds buffet the house,
warmth is filling the rooms
as the furnace starts up,
knowing this year
its job is just beginning

my new jacket

red as the heart of a fire,
its grey lining is meant to keep
me warm as toast in cold weather,
but not in freezing winter

walking in the brisk morning air
i wear my warm wool cabby's hat
with the short overhang,
shielding my eyes from the sun

a new neighbor brings out
her garbage can waving at me
as I briskly walk past her house;
she only moved in a few days ago

a strong gust of wind blows
her bathrobe open exposing
a sheer nightgown;
bringing smiles
and soft laughter
to my face

i enjoy my morning walks

nature

dashing about, it is a blur of four
tiny brown feet scampering
in the yard
from one end to the other,
never stopping to rest

winter is almost here;
the chipmunks are getting
ready to hunker down,
but not in my garage this year

peppermint soaked cotton balls
strategically placed by the doors,
with cayenne pepper sprinkled along
the side walls too; to keep them out

i have no problem sharing with nature
or with anyone else for that matter;
i already experienced sharing
with them once, that was enough

they belong outside
i belong inside
and i will try to keep it
that way…maybe;

you never know the future

are there still ten?

obviously, some of us do not have to do
all ten commandments;
there are a few we can ignore
as our elected leaders do

we can hold money up as
a deity, something to worship,
mimicking a recognized religious god

preemptively bomb countries into
submission with atomic bombs,
and kill innocent civilians;
if we have them, why not use them?

forget our marriage vows,
 if she is hot go for it;
adultery is now permitted
especially if a newborn is home

oh, and stealing is also acceptable.
if someone works for you,
no need to pay workers; keep the
money and steal their labor

coveting a neighbor's property
is now approved; using
eminent domain allows you
to build a bigger building

plus lies are also sanctioned,
fake news and false witness to
events which never happened;
all is good now, no sweat…

*how many commandments
does the religious right have left?*

death

looking at the trees lined up
on my street with multicolored limbs;
their beauty filling my eyes,
they are standing straight and tall;
reaching to the sky, then letting go

there are many colored leaves in this world,
and your small one floats lightly in the air;
wending its way down from the top

you flit to the left then to the right,
up and down subject to breezes
beyond your control

eventually either landing softly,
or plummeting to the ground,
to rest forever;
soon…

your existence
will be forgotten

Saturday

what a miserable day it is,
high winds and whipping drizzle
blasting my face with heavy rain-
a typical fall weather day

gone are hot summer ones
with scantily clad girls
tanning on a beach towel-
with the sun smiling down

today i see them in warm coats
with a sweater underneath,
and a hat pulled down tight
against the driving wind

the best part of today
is when i woke up early,
flipped my eyes wide open
and had another day of life

for my bride

i can't wait till tomorrow
when I will again hold you
in my arms

today's not enough
for me you are so dear
to my heart

i waited so long
for you to come
into my life

my heart
is wide open
to embrace
you in my soul

our future is unknown,
our years have crept so fast,
my heart belongs
to you my dear,
for now,
and forever

illness

our friend is sick
and has a fever;
taken to the hospital,
she is treated for dehydration
and infused with antibiotics

although we want to visit
we decide not to go;
when someone is ill
they feel lousy,
and want to be left alone
to heal,
not entertain

we stayed away
not because we do not
care for her

but because we love her;
does that make sense?

60's flower child

she is a stargazer
out of step with time

in her own world
looking far ahead

although her two feet are
stuck tightly in today

while she's preaching
for peace and love

they spew vile hate at her-
against her words of kindness

extraction day - a circle of life

waiting to go to the dentist
i hear the garbage trucks outside
picking up peoples soiled waste

what, I ask myself, do dentists
do with the silver and gold from
extracted teeth they pull?

i doubt they throw it in the trash
or smelt it in their back utility room;
maybe, they have an empty coffee can?

now, i wonder, where are they
going to place my tooth
which will be extracted?

will it be saved with the valuables,
or discarded with empty coffee
cups and sandwich bags?

honestly, i think it'll soon be
going for a ride in a big truck
filled with people's refuse

not only will i lose a tooth
but the tooth fairy does too!
and i'm out a tooth and cash

funeral for Farley

the line of crows
are perched
on a tree limb-
high above the desolate
windblown cemetery
patiently waiting;
intently watching
two men below
digging deep
into the cold, hardened earth

the birds are hoping
for a frightened small mouse
to frantically dash out
of a safe earthen burrow
for their next meal

while i am tearfully holding a box of ashes
watching them
above and below
as I keep my long time faithful companion
in my freezing hands
remembering his warmth

the only one in life
who gave me unconditional love
while i wait for the men to finish their work;
throwing shovel after shovel
over their broad shoulders
building a small mountain of rich virgin soil

as the biting Autumn wind
pecked at my reddened cheeks;
i notice, nearby, red and gold leaves

clinging
as long as they can
to the tall
dappled
brown barked
denuded ornamental trees
as the short bushes above the graves
sway back and forth;
dancing on the rows of long-forgotten souls

finally letting go
of their tight grip under duress;
the lifeless leaves
float softly in the air
leaving their tree of life
as they are blown about
not in control of their destiny;
landing on the bottom
of the newly dug grave

making a colorful
thick
plush
bed of death
welcoming me in;
as i kneel
to place Farley's polished mahogany box
filled with his ashes
gently on them

sealing both their fates for eternity

one day's mail

quietly sitting on the grass
half asleep, he lifts his head
when the mail truck stutters
down the block;
stopping at every house

as the truck pulls up to his home
he stands, alert and watching,
as the uniformed postman
extends his hand out the window
to stuff letters in the mailbox

growling, exposing his teeth,
he lunges forward only to be stopped
by the grey chain link fence;
while the mail truck continues to lumber
to the next home a few feet away

satisfied he protected his turf
his muscles relax;
he sits down
on his favorite spot
below the tree,
then begins to lick himself;
and life goes on

driving for romance

while driving on the road of love
i realize it is not a one-way street
but actually two lanes;
one going and one coming

the one-way street is a dead end
for a lasting romance; you must
be able to give as well as receive
kindness,
compassion,
and empathy

about her brother

she cried
as she read her poem,
her emotions raw,
unleashed;
escaping
from deep within her heart,
with flowing tears
a witness

honestly
releasing her feelings
about his untimely death
at such a young age,
for us to experience
with her

Sunday shopping

it was a sunny day that morning
when the friends met after church,
and decided to go shopping
just for giggles and a laugh

the girls drove downtown
to their favorite clothing store-
whizzing around the racks
with smiles from ear to ear

outside two cars crashed
with tempers flaring high;
it happened in a carry state
and gunshots rang outside

crashing through the windows
the bullets found their marks-
not the ones intended for
but two happy girls did die

if you look up sometimes
you might hear
giggles and a laugh
from somewhere up high,
as two angles fly by

on a bright and sunny day

she's dating again

*"i never thought at sixty-two
i'd be sleeping with three men"*

life has many twists and turns
many of which
are beyond our control

she was married for forty years
to her childhood sweetheart,
they were meant to be forever

life, unfortunately, has no guarantees
and stuff happens beyond our control-
sometimes good, sometimes not

he was strong and fit and
she was the one with the illness,
but she is here, and he is not

sometimes…

life sucks

after all these years

he didn't hate his mother,
or his religion either;
it was an emotional barrenness
held towards them both-
although she did all the usual things
one could ask a mother to do;
and the belief in a deity also evaporated-
not to be confused with a proud heritage

it could all be boiled down to one day years ago
when he was ten; he remembers it well

sitting on a hard wooden bench outside
the religious school principal's office -
while his parents were inside
trying to get him admitted; he was bored

finally the principal and his parents
walked out the frosted glass door-
the principal asks him a question
and a flip answer is given

the admission slip is torn up and thrown
in the wastebasket in front of everyone-
incensed, when they arrive home
his mother beat him with a leather belt

since that day he would mouth the words
expected of him, both to her and God,
but there were no feelings attached to them

an emptiness enveloped him
never to be replaced

the moth, the woman, and me

the bright flame of the candle
 is intense and hot,
  yet it draws the moth to it-
  flying into the heat
   not able to withdraw itself
    from an addiction like desire
     to go into the light-
      and prevent its demise

i notice a young woman
walk by me-
whose arms
are tattooed from wrists to shoulders
with multiple drawings in handcrafted colors;
a small silver ring pierced through her nose
and gold earrings outlining the ear-
with two
bright red,
thick,
pouty,
inviting lush lips
  beckoning me;
wearing tight
torn jeans
hugging her beehive curves,
accentuating
every movement with
every step she takes-
and tussled,
windblown,
long brown hair
flowing
down her back

i am drawn to her
wild girl image-
against all my intuition
and knowledge
gained from maturity
and marriage
not to approach her,
yet i do so willingly…
not able to help myself;
i don't know why

December 24th

driving on the Atlantic City Expressway
going to the casinos
intending to gamble,
and eat at the five-star restaurants,
is a caravan
of Jews and Asians
on Christmas Eve

entering the city
traffic lights
hold up the constant flow,
as i notice
standing on each corner
of the intersection
groups of women

sparsely dressed
they approach the cars
exposing their wares,
trying to entice the occupants
to spend their cash
on them instead of the casinos

being near the Atlantic Ocean at night
the temperature is below freezing,
with a wind chill in the single digits;
but business is business
to addicts and whores

i can see their legs and arms
turning red from the cold breeze;
while they try to keep warm
by shaking their bodies
and boobs at us

they are black, white, and yellow;
with every color in-between
you might find in a crayon box;
i feel for them,
they are someone's daughter,
a child gone astray

on my way home
before i leave the city
i pull next to the curb;
three girls run over to me
asking me to party

i hand each a fifty dollar
food voucher from the casino
and wish them a Merry Christmas

as i drive away i glance
in the rearview mirror
to see two girls smile,
and wave goodbye to me;
the third waves
by flipping me
the bird

i smile,
laugh a little laugh
to myself,
knowing Santa
will put me
in the good boy
book tonight

a kiss

as a young man, I kissed many
meaningless girls on the lips-
not out of love, but for romance,
as a means to an end

i grew up in a family which was
loving and caring, yet not demonstrably;
we never kissed on lips or hugged.
lip kissing was for intense love only,
not intended for a parental type of affection

at fifteen grandma, the oldest child,
with her father already deceased
made a promise to her dying mother-
to care and protect her siblings.
once married she kept her promise
and brought them from Europe;
to escape hatred, hunger, and an orphanage

my grandmother was in a loveless
marriage of convenience.
she broke an engagement to a man
who brought her to America after
reneging on a promise to bring over her siblings.
she then married a man who said he would,
and kept his promise

she had two sons by him
and a daughter, my mother

during the hot New York summers my grandfather
went to hotels in the Catskill mountains; without her.
she was left in the city with her three children and
three siblings; while he schmoozed on vacation

mom was very close to grandma
as daughters usually are;
i was my mother's first and only son
and spent a lot of time with my grandmother

every day, for years, when I was in elementary school
my grandmother picked me up for lunch;
told me stories so I would eat,
while she smoked
unfiltered camel cigarettes,
drank Maxwell House coffee, black,
and listened to
As The World Turns on the radio

on grandma's deathbed
some of her grandchildren
were brought for a final goodbye;
i was the last one in

on my turn, i kissed her
on the cheek, as they did too;
as i raised from her bed
she placed her hand behind my head

i want a kiss she said;
my face was pulled to hers-
then she kissed me
on the lips

after the kiss,
she turned her head on the pillow,
closed her eyes

and died peacefully

absurdity

they go to church
praying to a god
who preaches
love,
charity,
and kindness to all

yet they want to
stop birth control
stop abortions
stop food stamps
stop welfare
stop free medical care

let them have their unwanted babies
let them worry about feeding them
let them watch kids get sick and die

because
they have a deficit to control
they have tax cuts to giveaway
they have to stop all "benefits."
they have a self-given righteousness

and on Sunday,
they have to go to church

The End

Other books by Elliot M. Rubin

A trilogy of police/adventure novels
    Hot Cash/Cold Bodies
    Kara Bennet - Vengeance
    Dead Girls Don't Die

Romance and Murder in Bensonhurst

Flash Fiction
    People Stories in 600 Words
     (as told by a raconteur)

Poetry
    Surf Avenue Girl and other poems
    Scrambled Poems from My Heart
    A Boutique Bouquet of Poems and Stories
    Rumblings of an Old Man
    flash pan poetry

Jewish Satire
    The Phartick Chronicles

www.CreativeFiction.net

www.ingramcontent.com/pod-product-compliance
Lightning Source LLC
Chambersburg PA
CBHW031657040426
42453CB00006B/333